Before Marriage: A Primer

Douglas A. Lawton

LIVITY BOOKS

Before Marriage: A Primer

Copyright © 2017 by Dr. Douglas A. Lawton

This book is copyrighted. All rights reserved. No portion of this book protected by this copyright may be reproduced in any form or by any means, electronic or mechanical, including photocopying and recording, or by any information storage or retrieval system without the written permission of the publisher.

ISBN 978-1-941632-33-8

Published by:
Livity Books LLC, West Palm Beach, Florida 33416

Table of Contents

	Preface	5
1	Health in Marriage	7
2	Communication in Marriage	13
3	Reflections on Life	21
4	Reflections on Love	27
5	Choosing a Partner	31
6	Negotiating Your Way	37
	Suggested Resources	53

Preface

Human beings are multidimensional creatures. We are spiritual, physical, intellectual, emotional and social beings. All these areas of personhood are connected to form an integrated being. Ill health in one area compromises the health of the person on the whole and as such may compromise the wellbeing and potential of a person connected to him or her by marriage. Since the whole person has to be accepted and interacted with on a daily basis, it is imperative that couples get to know each other in the aforementioned areas before committing to marriage.

Getting to know each other takes time and involves asking questions that are appropriate. If the right questions are not asked, couples may never know what they are getting into and may start out in a deficit. Couples often rush into marriage failing to ask questions crucial to marital success. Instead, assumptions are made, which when proven untrue, tend to send the couple into shock, resulting in much drama, dysfunction, and for some, separation or divorce. It goes without saying that if the right questions are not asked, one will never get the right answers.

Years of preparation and hard work go into being qualified to pursue a career in most fields. After that there is examination and on-going certification. In some cases, a license may be involved in order to operate legally, plus refresher courses to keep the professional up-to-date with the most current information in their chosen field.

As difficult and expensive as pursuing a career is, people are committed to staying the course because it means opportunities to make a living and the ability to achieve other important goals. Unfortunately, the same level of commitment does not obtain in marriage.

The information in this book is intended to facilitate the conversation on marriage and enable couples to better ascertain whether or not they are suitable for each other as partners in marriage.

Adequate knowledge is a crucial part of the preparation for marriage. The partner a person chooses may help one up or take one down. In order to enhance the preparation for family life, a separate tool in the form of a questionnaire is suggested. The questionnaire confronts issues often overlooked in courtship due to ignorance or lack of courage, and teases out other questions relevant to the formation of a viable long-term relationship. It is recommended that the questionnaire be used in the context of premarital counseling. Additionally, it is the author's intent that it is administered and interpreted by a qualified counselor. Other resources to enhance preparation for marriage and enhance preservation are suggested at the end of the book.

1
Health in Marriage

When we talk about health in marriage, we are speaking in relative terms. Health is relative to the type and level of intelligence in operation. Consequently, there are various degrees of health. Moreover, it is possible to be healthy in some areas and not in others. Although an ideal worth striving for, perfection is impossible. Everyone is a work-in-progress. The goal should be holistic development.

Holistic development or health in marriage involves six chief areas of concern: the spiritual, physical, psychological, financial, social and communication skills of the couple. When a couple relates well along these lines, goals are more likely to be accomplished and desires are more likely to be fulfilled.

Health in marriage is dynamic and is not the same for everyone. We all have limitations, strengths, and weaknesses, and therefore operate at different levels of competency.
Marital health means intelligence-based growth. As stated earlier, health is relative to the level of intelligence in op-

eration. Intelligence is to be developed in a number of areas. As the couple journey toward marriage, intelligence needs to be developed spiritually, physically, psychologically, and socially. Since not much may be accomplished without money, and because communication plays a vital role in everything, intelligent communication and financial intelligence must be included in the discussion. Health in all these areas impacts the wellbeing of the marriage.

Relationship growth is based on knowledge. In addition to really getting to know your partner (your main stake holder), developing intelligence in other areas is crucial to marital success.

In the main, people fail, not because they lack integrity, but due to faulty assumptions and ignorance. Simply put, there is an intelligence gap in important areas of the relationship. Add impatience or unwillingness to endure the learning curve, and disaster is guaranteed.

As far as relationships go, beginning in the home, knowledge is passed on from one generation to the next via the behavior modeled by significant others. In addition to moral values, the impartation of knowledge involves other areas such as family life, food preparation, modes of communication and occupational skills.

Learning takes place informally through interaction with various social groups, and formally through schools, churches and vocational centers, for example. The efficacy of what is learned is determined by the nature of intelligence. If the intelligence is sound, growth will be positive; if unsound, growth will be negative.

People who succeed at marriage usually have two things in common: firstly, a mentor or good role model; secondly, they are committed to developing intelligence in that area.

Responsibility for health in marriage is shared
Responsibility for the health of the marriage is that of the couple. Each spouse shares responsibility for health in the marriage. If both are healthy, the marriage will be healthy. Both therefore need to focus on personal development and on achieving maximum health in all areas of concern. To be healthy, each person needs to be engaged in motivating and encouraging each other. It takes two to tangle and two to tango.

Intelligence is important in every area of life. Individuals, institutions, governments, and societies fail, not because they are not well-intentioned, but chiefly due to ignorance. Ignorance in any area of life can create problems and exacerbate existing ones. Let us now take a closer look at the need for intelligence in the chief areas of concern.

Spiritual
Since God who is Spirit, is the Creator and Inventor of marriage, spirituality plays a crucial role in marriage and life in general. It is therefore imperative that the created pursue a personal relationship with the Creator, and seek to embrace spiritual laws. A personal relationship with God does not only connect human beings to God spiritually. It also provides meaning and enables moral centering.

Everyone needs a moral compass, and everyone needs a sense of meaning and purpose.

Although a person may be moral without God, spirituality enables meaning and makes morality more sustainable. Moral centering is necessary to anchor the couple morally. Spirituality is necessary to inform the character of marriage; it nurtures and protects it. Thus spiritual intelligence is needed.

Physical
Physical well-being is important. Besides sex, the couple is obliged to take care of the physical needs of each other, such as food, shelter, clothing, and safety. Any form of ill-health resulting from lack in these areas may cause a strain on the marriage and undermine the relationship. Abuse of one's body by self or others must therefore be resisted. Life in all its beauty may be more fully enjoyed and much more may be accomplished when physical health is the experience. Among other things, being healthy physically involves proper exercise, rest, the appropriate diet, as well as intentionally addressing any medically-diagnosed condition. Intelligence, related to physical well-being is a critical component of the marriage relationship.

Psychological
Psychologically, the couple is part of a team, whose interactions affect each other emotionally, intentionally and unintentionally. In addition, influences from outside also affect members of a family. What affects one member usually affects others and, by extension, significantly affects their emotional wellbeing. In order to remain healthy

and achieve success, one must therefore guard against emotional distress and abuse, irrespective of the source or trigger. In this regard, emotional intelligence is crucial.

In addition to emotional development, psychological health includes cognitive development. Cognitive development refers to the mental action or process involved in acquiring knowledge and understanding, involving our thoughts, experiences, and senses. Therefore intellectual stimulation and growth must be attended to along the way.

Social
Socially, the couple becomes part of a network. Though not exclusively, this involves members connected biologically, inclusive of members of the extended family. The extended family may include friends bonded together in love and affection for each other. Health in the family system is crucial. One needs to support the other and help members of the network advance in ways that build up the family system on the whole making it stronger. Meaningful connections are not only crucial in terms of enabling social mobility or success in business, but are also important in terms of spiritual, physical, psychological, social, and financial wellbeing as well as involvement by way of intelligent communication. Couples need to be adaptable to the social and cultural nuances each partner bring to the table.

The social network has tremendous possibilities for evil and for good. Therefore growth in social intelligence must be included. Social support is crucial in every area of life, especially as the couple becomes seniors and in need of elder care.

Financial

Financial intelligence also plays a major role in the stability and success of every marriage. There is a cost attached to family life: bills must be paid, and future needs should be anticipated and prepared for. Accordingly, income needs to be generated to offset current and future expenses.

Not everyone is financially intelligent. People have different views on money. The majority is financially challenged in one way or another, some due to no fault of their own. In the meantime, financial distress is a major cause of marital dysfunction and divorce everywhere. A focus therefore on financial intelligence is necessary.

Since communication permeates every area of life and is a vital part of the marriage experience, the focus of the next chapter is communication in marriage.

2
Communication in Marriage

Knowledge is critical to human development. But how is knowledge received or apprehended? This is a factor of intelligent communication – the ability to communicate clearly and effectively information, concepts, thoughts, feelings, etc. without violating the rights of others. Intelligent communication includes: knowledge, sensitivity, active listening, truth, straightforwardness, respect and self-control.

Communication is not a one-sided affair. At the most basic level, it involves a sender and receiver. The receiver must be able to understand the message being communicated and meaningfully contribute to the discourse. As such, too wide a gap intellectually may pose a problem in terms of a couple's ability to relate to each another, and by extension may impact the overall development of the relationship.

Intelligent communication is important in every area of life, especially in family life. Couples unavoidably share a common space and will very likely and hopefully have much to talk about. Communication should be easy and unforced.

Be sensitive
Communication is inevitable and is not a one-way street. In addition to communicating with words or verbally, couples also communicate with their emotions and nonverbally. Body language sometimes betray what words are saying. There needs to be congruence. On the other hand, words are sometimes charged with emotions, negatively and positively. Negative emotions disrupt the communication process. Sometimes it is not what is said that is harmful but how it is said.

Understanding at the emotional level is just as important as understanding at the intellectual level. Since communicating at the feeling level is just as important as communicating at the intellectual level, developing one's mental and emotional intelligence is crucial.

Moreover, for conversations to be meaningful, a person need to communicate at the level of your partner's ability to grasp what you are trying to say. Furthermore, your partner should be interested in what you are saying. Couples should be able and willing to participate in the conversation.

In terms of communication, it is impossible for a person to meet all the communication needs of a spouse, as interests do not always collide and communication needs invariably differ. Not everyone is interested in the minute details of an event, and certain types of communication are better with a girlfriend, boyfriend or colleague.

Be balanced in how much you communicate, how often you communicate, and what you communicate. Some partners leave the marriage because of a spouse who talks too little; and others because of a spouse who talks too much. Be in tune with your spouse and be sensitive to your spouse's need to communicate.

A very important part of communication is silence and the need to observe this, respect it and allow each other to experience it. Learning the value of silence and making allowance for quietude should be embraced as an enhancing element of the relationship. Not much may be achieved amidst the din.

A person needs space to think, to get in touch with their inner self and to listen to the "small" voice of the Spirit. Silence is golden to those who appreciate and know how to utilize it. Interpreting silence is also important. Silence does not necessarily mean consent and sometimes speaks louder than words.

Communicate with problem-solving as a goal
When there's a problem, instead of drawing conclusions and judging your partner, it is imperative you exercise enough care to confront your partner, making every effort to accomplish this in a sensible and appropriate manner. Check your assumptions before accepting anything as fact and consider possible interpretations of facts before making conclusions. Do not entertain or encourage gossip. Do not be gullible. Ask questions and take time to ascertain the facts. Much of what you hear may bear no resem-

blance to facts, may be just speculation, may be misinterpretation or misrepresentation and may be inimical to your best interest. Facts have different interpretations, therefore consider alternatives.

Speak respectfully and positively
Do not belittle, talk down to, or speak patronizingly. How you say what you say is just as important, or may even be more important than what you say. Sensitivity to temperaments, moods, and stressful situations, for example, should inform the approach and timing, as well as the where and what of communication. Learning to read body language is helpful in providing clues regarding what your partner is thinking and feeling. Look for agreement or disagreement between verbal and nonverbal language. If verbal communication does not match the nonverbal, then you know you have a problem to solve.

Watch your lips what they speak. Spoken words have a life of their own and, like a spent arrow, can never be retrieved. Words spoken have the power of life and death, and therefore should be weighed carefully. Be humble. It's not always about who is right and who is wrong. Look at the big picture.

Confronting some people about wrongdoing will not always prove fruitful except to create awareness that you are in the know. A spouse may hear "I'm sorry" just to avoid consequences or in order to make the offended feel better. Most people who apologize for doing wrong are not truly sorry for what they did. They are only sorry for being found out and for the likely consequences. Use pattern to judge behavior, not isolated incidences. Albeit, a sincere apology goes a long way in settling disputes. To be truly sorry is not only to regret; it is, most importantly, to go in a new direction.

Despite the need for an apology, forgiveness is often the most important therapeutic intervention strategy. One should first learn to forgive one's self. If wrong has been done, a person should not go around feeling sorry for self and punishing one's self. Whether or not forgiveness is received from others, it is important that, without justifying inappropriate behavior, a spouse is charitable and gracious toward one's self.

The greatest gift a person can give or receive is the gift of forgiveness. The forgiver releases a pain too hard to bear, and the forgiven a burden too heavy to carry. Forgiveness assures liberty – the freedom to love again, trust again, and live again. Taking ownership or accepting responsibility is the first step. The second step is to make it right with God. The third step is to make it right with others. Of course, in order to go forward, a person must commit to change. Change is often the most convincing proof of being sorry for deeds of the past and of commitment to the marriage.

Listen actively
Listen to understand, not to rebut. Remember the world is not always as you see it, and everyone has a right to their own opinion. If you wish to be heard, you need to respect your spouse's opinion and give him/her a chance to speak

without interruption.

Interrupting a person while he/she communicates an opinion indicates the listener does not value or appreciate what the speaker is saying. This may lead to feelings of being bullied or disrespected. Disrespect undermines a spouse's ability to influence outcomes. One needs to try to see the other person's point-of-view and respectfully acknowledge differences of opinion. A person can disagree without being disagreeable. Awareness of one's own perspective and the ability to see things from the other person's point-of-view goes a far way in managing and minimizing disputes.

Be truthful and assertive
Learn to speak up for yourself. Most people will abuse you if they feel you are unable or unwilling to defend yourself. Furthermore, people are often misled by silence. Silence is invariably interpreted as consent, agreement or weakness. People will never know what you are thinking or feeling unless you express it. Bottling up will eventually cause an explosion and could be fatal. So express your thoughts and feelings before reaching boiling point.

Exercise self-control
Speak your mind. But being candid does not mean you should be unkind or disrespectful. You need to be brave enough to confront and care enough to do so respectfully. If the truth needs to be told or there is need to defend yourself, wait for the appropriate time, and speak your truth in love. You can be assertive without being aggressive, argumentative or combative; plus you can be candid and respectful at the same time.

In order to avoid misunderstanding and further abuse, mediation may be necessary. Do what you must. Remember, you always have a choice. You can choose to facilitate inappropriate behavior or motivate appropriate behavior. Choose wisely.

Never allow people's opinion, fear, or shame to intimidate you in accepting an unhealthy situation. Do not react. Act intelligently.

3
Reflections on Life

Many people go through life without doing any serious reflection. The same things are done over and over again, without considering why. Adding insult to injury, we keep doing the same things in the same way while expecting different results. Some say this is insanity, and they are right.

It is easy to get stuck in our traditions and time warps. Because other ways of viewing the world and of doing things are not part of our perceptual lens, traditions remain unchallenged and other possibilities go untapped. We accept the status quo and are afraid to leave our comfort zone. Yet we complain of boredom and of being unfulfilled.

Unless we take time to reflect on what we are doing, why we are doing it, where we are, and where we need to be going, a lot will be missing from our lives. We will miss out on the joy of life, miss important lessons, a tremendous number of opportunities and miss our destiny. Failure to do serious reflection along the journey will contribute to missteps, leaving us stuck, and "sick and tired of feeling sick and tired."

Here are a few things I have learned along the way: Doing life is like learning to walk: you take one step at a time and you take risks. When you fall, you get up and keep going. With each step your skill improves, so does your confidence and sense of security.

There will be unfolding and learning as you go along. Life is a journey. Take it one day at a time or one step at a time.

If you never take risks, you are unlikely to lose anything; but you will not gain anything either.

You do not have to be perfect to be right, have a perfect plan to attempt anything new, or have the perfect circumstance to do the right thing.

Instead of being paralyzed by fear, you need to keep trying. If you learn from each mistake, eventually you'll get it right.

Making a mistake is not necessarily a reflection on your character, but it certainly makes a statement as to whether or not you have pluck – the willingness to experiment and the courage to follow through on your desires or beliefs.

Whatever you take away from your experiences determines the sum of your equation: whether your life is positive or negative, or whether you succeed or fail. It also affects how you relate to similar experiences and how you relate to people who remind you of those experiences.

It is not the negative experiences that stump us; it is our interpretation, and our unwillingness to adapt and learn from those experiences.

Sometimes intelligence-based intervention is needed – in order to help us get a better perspective, to facilitate the healing process and to make us whole again.

Life is about being your best and doing your best. It is also about helping others to be their best and to do their best.

You do not have to always agree to get along, but you need to get along in order to move along.

When the seasons of life face you, embrace them. It's time to celebrate, not negotiate. Just as there are seasons associated with the natural environment (spring, summer, autumn, winter), there are seasons associated with the lifespan of an individual and with the lifespan of a marriage. "To everything there is a season." (Eccl. 3:3).

Be cautious about people who try to impress you with material possessions, and do not be anxious to accept gifts.

Look beyond the gift to the intention. Not every gift is from God. The devil has his counterfeits. Some gifts originate in divine intervention; others in diabolic circumvention. Some gifts are intended to help you; others to hinder you. "All that glitters is not gold." (Sir William Shakespeare)

Learn to appreciate the little things as well as the big things in life. You are more likely to receive the "big things" if you show respect and appreciation for the "little things."

When you show appreciation, you not only encourage the joy of giving, you encourage the joy of receiving: and you virtually ensure the act is repeated.

Balance sentimentality with pragmatism. If a thing is broken, fix it; if lost, find it; if useless, discard it; if dead, bury it; if you can't have it, forget it; if life-threatening, run or kill it; if life-giving, embrace and defend it.

People may add value to you, but under no circumstances should you allow yourself to be devalued.

Do not look to the fleeting things of life or people for your sense of security; neither should you confuse ancestry, activity, status or possessions with your identity. Anchor yourself in God – the Rock that cannot and will not be moved. Everything and everyone else has their time and season.

Do not take the joy out of living with pretense of perfection, and do not frustrate yourself and others with unreasonable demands. While striving for growth, make allowance for your own imperfections and that of others. Treat others as you would like to be treated.

You cannot control for everything. Accept the fact that God alone is in total control, knows everything about anything and able to accurately predict outcomes all the time.

If a person is underperforming in an area, maybe there is a deficit. This could be lack of resources or lack of knowledge. Try bridging the gap between the underperformance and the deficit and you may have a winner.

It is not enough to identify a problem. It is however, more than enough to focus on the solution, on being less critical and being more helpful.

Although awareness is important, no one succeeds by identifying problems. We succeed by being able to solve them. Be solution-oriented.

If the grass seems greener on the other side, maybe it is because the people on the other side are willing to put in the work and you are not.

Live within your means. Borrow to invest, not to consume.

No one enters the world without affecting it in one way or another. The difference you make in the world is your legacy and the only thing you get to take with you on your way out. Your legacy may be good or evil and only you can determine that.

What others say about you is not nearly as important as what you say about you. And "actions speak louder than word."

While on earth, you get to make an investment in heaven or in hell. You will be rewarded in proportion to where you place your investment and the level of your investment. Prosperity is not about how much you have gained for yourself. It is about whether or not you use your wealth to enrich and empower others to prosper.

4
Reflections on Love

Choosing a partner for marriage is more than an intellectual exercise. It also involves the engagement of emotions. Cognition of the heart needs to be balanced with cognition of the mind. As true love involves the will, emotions and intellect, love needs to be intelligently excited and intelligently directed. This chapter will briefly discuss what love is not and what love is, and will make a distinction between romantic love and being in love.

What love is not
Love is not lust. Some people confuse love with lust. Essentially, lust is ingratiating and selfish; it seeks sexual fulfillment without commitment and without genuine interest in the object of its desire.

Love is not infatuation or obsession. Infatuation is a flight of fantasy, and is short-lived. Obsession is a fix of fantasy; it is based on compulsion or uncontrolled desire without respect for the wishes of the object of affectation.

Love is not a static emotion. Love is dynamic; it can grow and can be diminished. Love may flourish when nurtured, wither when neglected, and may be misdirected and redirected.

Love is not something that may be arranged, although the introduction of kindred spirits is sometimes necessary to create the spark and ignite the flame. Although it is possible to fall in love at first sight, you may need several sightings to love intelligently and to stay in love.

What love is
Love is a process of endearment based on laws of attraction. Love in the context of marriage is a two-way street. It is not a one-sided affair. The essence of love is commitment to the welfare of another. In romantic relationships, love focuses on mutual desire and mutual fulfillment. It focuses on mutual interest, not self-interest; and is concerned about the total wellbeing of one's partner. Love is also the unconditional acceptance of another. In addition, despite the emotional connection, love is fundamentally a matter of choice, hence the need for intelligence.

Loving your partner is not the same as being in love. It is possible for the relationship to get stale, to lack fire or excitement, although there may be commitment to the marriage. Commitment to each other, and by extension to the marriage, is enhanced by the couple being in love.

How do you know when you are in love?
Romantic love is passion inflamed by desire thereby enabling, empowering, and fulfilling each other. You know you are in love when the object of your affection

(physically, symbolically or imaginatively) excites you beyond measure, filling you with intense joy.

You know you are in love when there is intense longing to be in the presence of someone, wanting to share space, time, resources and your whole being with him/her. You know you are in love when you truly care for the total well-being of a person.

The next chapter addresses the importance of choosing the right partner.

5
Choosing a Partner

Marriages are not made in heaven. Marriages are ordained by God but are made on earth. Earth and heaven agree only when the will of man agrees with the will of God. God does not choose for us. He gives us the ability to choose for ourselves. From creation, human beings have been endowed with volition – the ability to make choices. Our choices determine whether we enjoy marriage in all its beauty or endure it as a duty.

The path to marriage is relatively easy but the road becomes more complicated afterward. Since Adam, as recorded in the book of Genesis of the Bible, human nature has been corrupted. Some contributing factors to this are: the complexity of human personality, the emotions of love that invariably affects judgement, personal history, imperfect or non-existent role models, as well as current trends redefining and undermining marriage. In addition, people are not always transparent. Thus, what we see is not always what we get.

Before Marriage: A Primer

Success in marriage begins with personal readiness and the person you choose to journey with you. A good start increases your chance of finishing well. So preparation is very important. Preparation should have begun long before a person sets eyes on a potential partner. Preparation is the foundation on which your house is built. If the foundation is solid, your marriage will be strong. If not, there is greater likelihood of it tumbling down. At best, though not insurmountable, you will have a lot of problems along the way.

Try to establish friendship before embarking on courtship. As a friend you stand a good chance of knowing the real person – before intelligence and intuition are overwhelmed by emotion, and before true love is undermined by untamed passion. You may also get to know other friends and associates through unguarded and *unsanitized* activities.

Make sure you want to get married for the right reason. Ask yourself, "Why do I want to get married?" "Are these reasons proper bases for marriage?" "Will they hold up five, ten or twenty years from now?" Marrying someone because you feel the need to rescue him/her or because you think you can change the person is not a good idea. Marrying someone because you are financially or otherwise insecure, or want a child are not good ideas either.

Make sure you are compatible. Although love is a solid foundation for marriage, it is possible to be in love with the wrong person. Compatibility is also crucial. Incompatibility will cause you to pull in opposite directions, eventually causing an unraveling.

Ask yourself:

1. Do I connect with this person physically, emotionally, intellectually, socially and spiritually?
2. Do we share the same values?
3. Do we have similar goals?
4. Are we compatible in areas that are significant to both of us?
5. Do we complement each other?

There are many areas in which compatibility is desirable, and there are many signs of incompatibility. In this regard, a Compatibility Questionnaire may prove useful.

Relationship consultant, Sheila Blagg, suggests couples should look out for the following signs when dating:

- You laugh at the same time.
- Your conversations have a natural rhythm.
- You can finish each other's sentences.
- You make eye contact comfortably and often, without thinking about it.

According to Blagg, a person should trust their heart and instincts. (http://www.huffington post. com/sheila-blagg/signs-of-ompatibilityyo_b_5838192.html?ncid=txtlnkusao yo_b_5838192.html?ncid=txtlnkusaolp00000592).

Focus on being the right person. Being the right person is just as important as finding the right person. If marriage is desirable, you need to prepare yourself. Don't wait until you start dating. If you want a job, you have to make yourself employable, right? Well that takes years of preparation, including hard work, money and other resources. You are more likely to be the right person for the job, if you had been adequately prepared. It is no different in marriage. If you land the job and you are unable to perform, you are going to make a mess of it. You increase your chances of succeeding, if you focus on being the right person. Focus on personal development.

In any relationship, you cannot reasonably demand or expect others have attributes you yourself do not possess, can you? Be the person you desire others to be in terms of character and the laws of attraction will conspire in your favor. Like attracts like.

Pay attention. Be careful to pay attention to what your prospect is saying, and remember that action speaks louder than words. The decision-making process may be enhanced if you pay attention not only to what your partner is saying but also to what others are saying. The list includes friends, relatives, professional counsellors and pastors, whom, by virtue of their experience and or training may provide additional insight and guidance. Sometimes being in love causes you to see through rose-colored glasses, and therefore may affect judgment. For not being intimately involved, other people may be more objective and thus able to add insight which eludes you, not only by virtue of your being in love but also because of inexperience. Always pay attention. Remember, in the final analysis the decision is yours to make, and the consequences yours to enjoy or endure, especially in circumstances when wedlock is deadlock.

Watch out for intergenerational afflictions. Physical sick-nesses and diseases are sometimes passed down from one generation to the next genetically. The same is true psychologically, thereby affecting intellectual and emo-tion-al wellbeing. A similar thing occurs spiritually and morally through the nurture received in the home and other socializing agencies such as religious cults. It is therefore not unusual for problems identified in preceding generations to manifest throughout the bloodline, like drug abuse and divorce, for instance.

Marry a whole person. You want to marry someone who is complete or whole – not someone who is incomplete, or someone viewed as your other half, better half, or lesser half. Otherwise, you will find yourself in a situation where there are unrealistic expectations. For example, one spouse looking to the other to make him/her happy and complete, and both receiving their sense of significance from each other. Being in an enmeshed relationship is not healthy.

You may need another person to complement you but you do not need someone else to complete you. You came into this world a complete human being. Interdependency is normal; codependency is another matter.

"Don't judge the book by its cover." A beautiful mind is far more important than a beautiful body.

Bear in mind the fact that everyone has baggage. It might be helpful to be aware of what's in the bag. Sometimes professional help is needed to sort it.

Much of the problem we face in relationships and in society at large is associated with esteem issues: people either thinking too highly of themselves or too low of themselves, reflected in behaviors and attitudes toward one another, observable mostly in how we communicate with one another. We need to guard against feelings of inferiority or superiority, and against the desire to manipulate and dominate.

Relationships succeed when the parties share a number of things in common, are on the same page on important matters, are doing things together and are healthy in areas that potentially affect the wellbeing of each other and that of the marriage on the whole.

6
Negotiating Your Way

Negotiating your way in marriage is challenging, particularly if due care was not taken in the selection of a partner in the first place, and more so for people who did not have a positive role model to emulate, or do not have a mentor. Diverse cultures, backgrounds, personality traits, quirks, and imperfections make the period of adjustment difficult. Negotiating your way involves a lot of learning and adjusting. It involves learning about yourself, learning about your partner, learning about what works and doesn't work, learning to adapt to changes, and learning to work smart or to do things differently. Learning the strengths and weaknesses of each other goes a far way in negotiating roles, in determining expectations and in allocating resources for growth.

Be a learner
Be a learner. If you can learn from others, like a good mentor, the learning curve will not be as long and expensive. Don't shoot the message because of the messenger, and don't shoot the messenger because of the message.

Facts are facts regardless of the source. In addition, you can learn from anyone. You can learn from people who have made mistakes, and you can learn from your own mistakes. Mistakes do not end anything unless you let them. In fact, they sometimes make you smarter and stronger. Success is often the flipside of failure. Focusing on mistakes often lead to incapacitation, anger and bitterness.

Focus on the learning opportunity and solution. Life is not about failure. Failure is guaranteed when you stop learning and stop trying. There is a solution to every problem. Greatness is not measured by mistakes, but by resilience, by the things endured, and by the obstacles overcome in order to succeed. Making mistakes mean a person needs to try harder and work smarter. That's all there is to it. For sure, it is less expensive to learn from the mistakes of others. However you learn, make sure you learn. Otherwise, you will continue to be schooled by the University of Hard Knocks or pay dearly in some other institution.

Never stop learning. You can never know enough and you are never too old to learn. In this regard, your nurturing environment is crucial. If unable to surround yourself with good mentors, surround yourself with good books. No one succeeds without appropriate education or learning.

Be smart

Marriage is a huge investment and perhaps the biggest you'll ever make. It can make or break you, so invest wisely. Like any investment, it has risks and rewards. This is all the more reason for due diligence, constant assessment and the deploying of resources, including quality time, to make it work. Although there is no such thing as a perfect match, success in marriage begins with the intelligent, well-informed choice of a partner. Choose wisely.

Be a thinker
Take time to ponder, reflect and ask questions. It is not what we see or hear that makes fools or liars of us. It is the assumptions we make and how we interpret what is seen or heard. As much as possible, avoid making assumptions. Take time to assimilate the information you receive every day. Why? To see how it fits in the scheme of things, how it connects with what you already know, and with other bodies of knowledge. This will allow you to see how it may be applied in the present and in the future, and how it may affect your life and the lives of others. Take time for personal introspection. You may be surprised at the discovery. Take time to reflect on people, places and things. Be objective.

Be a whole person
Attend to those areas that make you well-rounded and healthy, the most important areas being your spiritual, psychological, physical, social, and financial wellbeing. Acknowledge strengths and weaknesses. Work on weaknesses and maximize your strengths.

Being whole does not mean perfection; it means commitment to holistic development. Commitment to holistic development enables growth in every area. It places you in a better position to add value to others and to receive value as well. Interdependence is natural and healthy; codependence is unnatural and unhealthy. In marriage, two halves do not make a whole. The spiritual mathematics is 1 + 1=1.

Be your own person
Oneness, however, does not mean you have to be the carbon copy of your spouse, or that you should walk in their shadow. Your sense of personhood and identity should not be morphed into that of your partner. Although one, you are still your own person. Being married does not mean you lose your own identity and individuality. Individual differences must be recognized, appreciated and celebrated. You can be a life partner without losing your life to your partner. Oneness has to with unity and singleness of purpose, not conformity to a person's whim, pattern or style of operation.

Sharing your life with a spouse is a good idea, but you need to have a life without her/him. Each partner needs space to grow, to breathe, to think, to enjoy his/her own company, to do things by one's self and for one's self, and sometimes with one's own friends and associates. Space is needed to connect with other minds and to enjoy their company without fear of compromise or jealousy; otherwise, marriage may be a hellish vortex. Self-identity and personal security is important, especially in a transient world – one in which commitment is fickle and there are no guarantees.

Be secured
You are God's masterpiece and therefore significant. As Creator, God is the best anchor on which your security should rest. As humans, we are prone to change. We are limited in our abilities, and our judgments are often im-

paired by faulty or corrupt lenses.

Look to God alone for security and significance. People value you based on your possessions and performance, or some other fleeting measure of success, and your significance rated accordingly. Moreover, no matter how much you have or how well-connected you are, none of these things can shield you from disaster. As far as people goes, they change, are susceptible to corruption, and are limited in their ability to keep you safe or protect you. Where possessions are concerned, manmade and natural disasters can strike and uproot you at any moment. Being unlimited in His ability, only God can keep you secured. Being unconditional in his love toward you, means that as far He is concerned, you are significant. Being your Creator, God can be trusted to secure and shield you.

The character of God is unchanging. In addition to being perfect, God knows you perfectly, loves you unconditionally and is unlimited in His ability to sustain and protect you. Yet you have a major role to play in that as well – in embracing God, believing what God says of you, and in fulfilling your God-given potential. Be a secure person. The greatest threat to your security is insecurity. Insecurity will manifest in inappropriate behavior; it will undermine mental health and the health of your relationship. Be secure.

Be positive
Health in marriage begins with a healthy mindset. A positive attitude will help you see the best in others, help you to look on the brighter side of things, and impel you to do your best and be your best. Positivity is the seed of crea-

tivity and the foundation of progress. Even if things are not going as planned or expected, a positive attitude will save you a lot of energy, spare you the effects of negative emotions, and facilitate a speedier recovery. A positive attitude can help you turn things around, or at the very least help you learn from your experience. Being positive does not mean being naïve or unrealistic. Positivity needs to be balanced with reality and sound judgment.

Be realistic
Be realistic. Expectations denied may lead to feelings of anger or resentment. The problem may be exacerbated if a spouse resorts to manipulation and control in order to have their way. Displays of control and manipulation will undermine the development of your spouse and restrict your own growth. It could result in you denying yourself the blessing of a supportive spouse along with his/her views and opinions, factors that could have proven invaluable. Being controlling and manipulative make going forward difficult.

Going forward is always difficult in such circumstances. Some couples may tolerate each other for financial reasons or because children are involved. A spouse may surrender personhood just to give a good impression or to avoid the "shame" associated with divorce. Still, others may either fight to fix the problem or opt out of the marriage altogether. At the end of the day, no self-respecting person will tolerate abuse indefinitely.

Part of the responsibility of being a couple is to promote wholeness, and to bring out the best in each other. Refusal to accept or call out inappropriate behavior is to enable and encourage it.

Many use the notion "for better or for worse" as cover for inappropriate behavior or as an excuse for not changing/growing. That's one reason a person should not get married with a view of changing a spouse into what one desires the spouse to be.

However, whatever the problem there is a solution. The solution may not be ideal, because it is sometimes impossible to find ideal solutions where sinful human beings are concerned.

It is not always what is said and done. Problems include attitudes and intentions needing to overcome. Problems are also due to ignorance and immaturity. This is all the more reason why one should not make rash decisions, and should seek professional help. If the marriage is broken, do your best to fix it. If unfixable, you can pray for a miracle or learn from your mistakes and move on.

Regardless, we can all agree that in order for any marriage to work, a couple needs to treat each other with love and respect; not as property or chattel.

Be goal-oriented
For there to be progress, decision-making strategies acceptable to both parties need to be discussed and implemented. Progress, however, takes time and is a factor of the nurturing environment. Albeit, a couple needs to decide what progress looks like, and plan toward its achievement. This means setting personal and family-centered

goals, and deciding on strategies to achieve them. Goals give you focus while strategies serve as guide steering you toward the achievement of your goals. Goals should be specific, measurable and time sensitive. Set long-term as well as short-term goals.

Since it is impossible to accomplish all your goals at the same time, you will need to prioritize. Deciding on what to do first or whose need to meet first can be challenging. Where your partner is concerned, learn to negotiate with each other and be open to change. Strive for a win-win solution. Where certain matters are concerned, learn to discern the difference between the important and the urgent, and attend to the most urgent matters first. There is need for agreement on what needs to be done, when it is to be done, why and how it is to be done, and who is responsible for doing what. It is also important to establish goals to help each other fulfil personal dreams.

Progress adds to feelings of success and releases positive energy in the relationship. Progress, however, does take time and is a factor of the nurturing environment. Be considerate and supportive.

Be considerate and supportive
Happiness in marriage may be enhanced when spouses help each other achieve personal goals and satisfy personal needs. Selfishness will destroy both you and your marriage. Working together to advance each other's interests serves to strengthen the bond and increases loyalty. Be considerate and helpful.

Criticize constructively
Consider how your words, attitudes and actions affect others, and put yourself in their position. "Do unto others as you would wish them to do to you." For example, some people are too stingy with praise and are just too critical in their views of life, rendering them too difficult to be with.

It is easier for them to find fault or give negative criticism than to congratulate someone or applaud a work well done. Instead of being mean, be sparing with criticism and generous with praise. Be your partner's biggest fan and cheer him/her along. Even if the person is not doing as well as expected, you can at least recognize effort. Recognizing their effort will often motivate the person to keep trying and will ultimately lead to increased improvement. A little encouragement goes a long way in helping both you and your spouse to go the distance. Putting each other down will lead to discouragement and failure. Marriage is about cooperation, not competition.

Nonetheless, constructive criticism is always in order. Criticizing your partner constructively is not a put down; it is a push in the right direction. It is a push up. In this regard, one needs to exercise maturity in embracing criticism designed to make one better or to improve one's performance.

Be happy
If you want to live a good and happy life, you have to choose your battles. "Don't sweat the small stuff," said Carlson. Avoid unnecessary stress. Enjoy life and be a pleasant person to live with. Seek to create an emotionally healthy climate for yourself and others. Seek to thrive

emotionally. In doing so, you will not only "win friends and influence people," according to Dale Carnegie, but conflicts will be diminished and goals will be more than likely achieved.

Happiness is your responsibility, not the responsibility of others. Important as other people are in the scheme of things, only you can make you happy and fulfilled. Happiness is a factor of *your* outlook and of the choices *you* make. Choose to be happy.

Be intentional and proactive
Make a conscious decision to be intentional in your approach to life and in the kind of atmosphere you create for yourself and others. If you leave anything up to chance, chances are it will never be achieved. Be proactive. You cannot predict everything or plan for everything but you can be proactive and prepare for most things.

Be disciplined and flexible
Whatever you set out to accomplish takes discipline and sacrifice. This means, if it becomes necessary, you have to be willing to give up something in order to get something. "You cannot eat your cake and have it." And remember, what works for one couple will not necessarily work for you. There are universal principles applicable to all, but both you and your partner are unique. Plus people do change, along with their motivations, tastes and desires. Navigating your way depends on how well you know each other and your openness to change. As you evolve, you will need to write your own play book, stick with the rules and revise where necessary.

Be patient
Someone once said "Rome wasn't built in a day." Although goals need to be accomplished and desires fulfilled, you need to be patient. Impatience will give way to discontent and will introduce negative emotions leading to ill-health in the relationship. You need to allow time for yourself and your partner to grow and not allow yourself to get caught up in the rat race. Everything has its time and season. Life is not about competition; it is about commitment to ideals which enable us to be our best and do our best. After we have done our best, the rest is up to God.

No marriage is trouble free
There is no marriage that is trouble free. Imperfect people are bound to act out their imperfections and unexpected life events can be extremely challenging. Invariably, there is failure not because of problems, but because of how problems are managed. Belief in the myth that if there are problems in the marriage it was never meant to be, can also lead to failure. The grass may be greener on the other side, but it still has to be mowed.

Be fair
If you have to fight, be fair; and keep the big picture in mind. Nitpicking and complaining about every little thing will not only destroy you emotionally, it will repel others, including your mate. Don't be a whiner. Be a winner. Whiners are irritators; winners are initiators and motivators. It goes without saying that people who are hypercritical are hypocrites: imperfect people demanding perfection of others. Putting down others is often a reflection of

one's own pathology. A wise person once said "attack the problem, not the person."

Never compare a spouse with another person, especially with your ex. Besides being unfair, it gives the impression that you are looking back with regret and has not fully moved on.

Avoid superlatives like "never" and "always." It is seldom true that a person has *never* done anything right or has *always* done something wrong. Furthermore, using such words often paints a gloomier picture than is the reality, and makes the situation seem hopeless. If you have to call out inappropriate behavior, stay in the present and be specific. Be willing to forgive, and avoid bringing up the past. If you are stuck in the past, you will never go forward.

Be honest
Some people take delight in pointing out the faults of others but are unwilling to confront their own demons. Instead of making excuses, accept responsibility for your own failures. Avoid smokescreens and blame shifting, and be humble enough to apologize when wrong.

Pick your battles
Be careful not to win the battle and lose the war, or win the fight and lose the marriage. Keep things in perspective. Winning is not everything. Sometimes you are not the best person to make the point; sometimes the point need not be made; and sometimes the time is not right.

Be solution-oriented

Because problems are to be expected in marriage, you need to improve problem-solving skills. Unfortunately, sharpening such skills includes solving problems that you yourself may have created. Be assured you will make your fair share of mistakes, no matter how hard you try. That's life. Imperfect matches do ignite and couples on occasion do have their fight. However, it is possible to control the flame and eventually put out the fire.

Internal and external conflicts are to be settled quickly. Unsettled disputes increase stress and affect the integrity of the mind and body. Ultimately, the integrity of the marriage is affected. It is much easier to put out a fire as soon as it has started than to attempt putting it out after it begins to spread.

Be solution-oriented. Just about anyone can identify problems, but it takes a special person to find solutions. If you focus on problems you are going to be stuck. Finding solutions is where the growth is.

Be mature and emotionally intelligent

We are emotional beings and must therefore learn to manage our emotions and master our moods. This takes maturity and emotional intelligence. Managing emotions is not easy because emotions deeply felt affect the whole person and is not easily discarded or compartmentalized. A person who is underdeveloped emotionally is a time bomb on legs and is not only capable of untold damage to others, but is also capable of damage to self and is severely restricted where growth in other areas of life is concerned. Emotional underdevelopment undermines personal growth and retards growth in interpersonal relationships at every level. This can only be countered be intentionally developing emotional intelligence.

Be content
One of the best decisions you could ever make is the decision to be content. Being content does not mean you lack ambition or that you are not progressive, but that you are willing to take things in stride, enjoy the good with the not so good, and that you are not controlled by life's circumstances. It means you are trusting in the One who alone is in full control of the vagaries of life and is able to work all things (both good and bad) together to advance the interest of His children. Life has its ups and downs. Be grateful for whatever life throws at you. You can choose to enjoy the ride or endure it until change comes.

Be the person you desire others to be
One cannot reasonably expect from others qualities he/she does not possess, can one? And a person cannot reasonably expect from others commitment or sacrifice he/she is unwilling to make.

Be the person you desire others to be. Attend to inner beauty and you will not have to worry about the competition. Being beautiful on the inside is the most brilliant of all achievements, because inner beauty not only makes you more desirable, it opens doors to achieve in other areas of life as well.

If you want to look pretty or be a really beautiful person, take care of your soul. There is no point in being pretty on the outside and ugly on the inside. Be genuinely beautiful. When there is beauty on the inside it will radiate outwardly. You become naturally attractive and become more desirable.

Do not waste your time trying to impress people
Living your life to impress or please others is a waste of time, a waste of energy, and a waste of limited resources. People can see behind the façade, and are inconsistent in their expectations. Although many are in the business of showmanship and are obsessed with making a good impression, life is not a show. It is what it is – reality. So be real. There is no point in trying to impress people or in competing with people in order to fit in or win approval. These are additional stresses you can ill-afford. If you are not self-directed, the desire to please or impress people will leave you extremely stressed and unfulfilled.

Avoid the rat race. The rat race will undermine your health and judgment. Set your own pace, and live your own dreams lest envy and jealousy overtake you and so cause you to destroy your house. When all is said and done, you will always have to deal with the real you – no matter where you go, what you do, or who you are with.

Keep it real. Be a genuine person and be sound in the choices you make. The odds of succeeding at marriage may be increased by making choices based on sound intelligence physically, spiritually, emotionally, socially, and financially.

Suggested Resources

Things I Wish I'd Known Before We Got Married by Gary Chapman

The 4 Seasons of Marriage: Secrets to a Lasting Marriage by Gary Chapman

The 5 Love Languages: The Secret to Love That Lasts Library Binding by Gary Chapman

How to Build a Better Spouse Trap by Hollis Green

Love & Respect by Dr. Emerson Eggerichs

His Needs, Her Needs: Building an Affair Proof Marriage by Willard Harley

Marriage on the Rock: God's Design for Your Dream Marriage by Jimmy Evans

Boundaries in Marriage by John Townsend

The Meaning of Marriage: Facing the Complexities of Commitment With The Wisdom of God by Timothy Keller and Kathy Keller

The Marriage Relationship by Douglas A. Lawton
Marriage Under Siege by Douglas A. Lawton

The Compatibility Questionnaire by Douglas A. Lawton

Twelve Rules for a Happy Marriage

1. Never both be angry at once.
2. Never yell at each other – unless the house is on fire.
3. Yield to the wishes of the other as an exercise in self-discipline – if you can't think of a better reason.
4. If you have a choice between making yourself or your mate look good – choose your mate.
5. If you feel you must criticize, do so lovingly.
6. Never bring up a mistake of the past.
7. Neglect the whole world rather than each other.
8. Never let the day end without saying at least one complimentary thing to your life's partner.
9. Never meet without an affectionate welcome.
10. Never go to bed mad.
11. When you've made a mistake – talk it out and ask for forgiveness.
12. Remember, it takes two to make an argument. The one who is wrong is the one who will be doing most of the talking.

- Author Unknown

Other Works by the Author

Marriage Under Siege
The Marriage Relationship
The Compatibility Questionnaire
Caribbean Crime and Violence
Spiritual Intelligence
Positive Vibrations
Values Vibes Workbook (One)
Values Vibes Instructors' Manual (One)
Meet Mr. Bigot

www.ingramcontent.com/pod-product-compliance
Lightning Source LLC
Chambersburg PA
CBHW061345040426
42444CB00011B/3089